# THE EYES
# OF ISAAC NEWTON

First published in 2017 by
The Dedalus Press
13 Moyclare Road
Baldoyle
Dublin D13 K1C2
Ireland

www.**dedaluspress**.com

ISBN 978 1 910251 27 0

Dedalus Press titles are represented in the UK by
Inpress Books, www.inpressbooks.co.uk,
and in North America by Syracuse University Press, Inc.,
www.syracuseuniversitypress.syr.edu.

Cover design by Pat Boran

The Dedalus Press receives financial assistance from
The Arts Council / An Chomhairle Ealaíon.

# THE EYES
# OF ISAAC NEWTON

IGGY McGOVERN

DEDALUS PRESS

## ACKNOWLEDGEMENTS

Acknowledgements are due to the editors of the following in which a number of these poems, or versions of them, originally appeared: *Acorn, Contrappasso (Aus.), Cork Literary Review, Irish Pages, Fermata, Flare Broadsheet, Magdalen Record (UK), Medical Journal of Australia (Aus.), Poetry Ireland Review, Southword, The Irish Times, The Lighter Craft: Poems for Peter Denman, The Pickled Body, Verbal Sun: Poems for the National Council for the Blind of Ireland, Windows 20 Years.*

The author wishes to thank the Tyrone Guthrie Centre and Varuna/The National Writers Centre of Australia for the provision of an exchange residency at the latter, and the Alexander von Humboldt Stiftung for supporting a research stay at The Centre for Literature and Natural Science (ELINAS) of the Friedrich-Alexander Universität Erlangen-Nürnberg, Germany.

# CONTENTS

Hypermetropia / 11
Alliteration / 12
Civilian / 13
The Male Line / 14
The Licensed Trade / 15
The Old Religion / 17
All My Eye / 20
Around the Village Pump / 21
Memoir / 23

II

From The F.X. Buckley Collection / 27
The Boy and the Caravaggio / 29
The Cross of Cong / 30
To Seamus Heaney in Heaven / 31
Air / 32
Rathlin Haiku / 34
Radio / 36
No Second Glance / 38
Love / 39

III

Pupil / 45
Second Chance / 46

Nightmare in The Women's Hall of Residence / 47
Time / 48
Colour / 50
At The Garden Pier, Atlantic City / 51
Music / 52
Horse / 54
Yeats Country / 56
Ulymericks / 57


IV


The Eyes of Isaac Newton / 65
Crossing The Uncanny Valley / 66
Motoring / 67
Science / 69
Quantum Clerihew / 71
His Cat / 73
Walking the Dog / 74


Notes / 75

*i.m.* Catherine Cotter

# I

'Eye for eye, tooth for tooth, hand for hand, foot for foot'
—Exodus 21:24

# Hypermetropia

Apocryphal, no doubt, the story of
the Dublin Tommy who had lost an eye
for King & Country during The Great War.
Invalided back home he refused
to leave the house until he was supplied
with a glass eye, one that would pass muster.
The first he judged the iris too large,
the next too small, another the wrong shade
of blue, and so on; it was many years
before he finally emerged to find
The Second City now in rebel hands
and all the garrison decamped; that eye
might have gone back with this direction:
"Request adjustment of far-sight correction".

# Alliteration

When the boy from the Soldiers' Cottages
allowed that I was a "Fuckin' Fenian"
and clipped my ear, I ran home faster
than speeding bullets, where, narrow-eyed,
my mother clipped the other ear
for using such "Lavatory Language".
And that was also the very same year
I trod on an up-turned six-inch nail
that pierced my sole, and my mother's heart,
as she set to work with Dettol and plaster,
all the while murmuring "Christ Crucified"!
And something else that formed a veil
like a gas cloud rolling over the rampart:
The murderous "Gang Green".

# Civilian

With each fresh bombardment
of beleaguered armchair positions
from the cooking-cleaning high ground,
he heads for the wardrobe shelter.

Hunkered down in the darkness,
he checks his meagre rations –
giant tin of Australian peaches,
unexploded champagne magnum,
rubbery gasmask and dwindling
eye-watering peppermints rustling
in Sunday's waistcoat pocket.

He would like to stay forever,
or at least till the fighting is over,
but the tramp of boots on the linoed stairs
have tracked him down again;
white flags have no meaning
for ten-year old flame-throwers:
"Burn, Daddy, burn"!

# The Male Line

Once, my father tried to rouse the fire
– my mother being gone to early Mass –
by pouring paraffin from an old jam-jar.
So focused on the task he seemed to miss
the presence of his young son in the arch
of his bent legs, a child too keenly drawn
to adult action, always on the search
for something new – well, he would soon learn
that when the heady vapour caught a spark
All Hell Broke Loose – My God, how I whinged!
But when in better light she would remark
that my fair eyebrows looked like they'd been singed,
I saved my breath to cool my porridge, and he
just winked to seal our first complicity.

# The Licensed Trade

## 1. Time

My father reconciles his books,
spectral in the Public Bar,
Sunday-shuttered, an after-smell
of porter and tobacco.
We are his only customers,
our silence bought with lemonade;
his sermon is the honest coin
he drops into the till.
Our eyes are on the bulbous set
above his desk, the soundless Brain
of Britain dappling his pate.
Time for Sooty? We should know
that best-run houses keep their clocks
a quarter-hour ahead.

## 2. The Mathematical Barman

The mathematical barman
lives in a world of his own;
he's calculating the average size
of the bubbles in each pint
or the different combinations of coins
in the right change from a fiver
or the time it takes a drop from the optic
to reach the slatted floor.
But the customers all love him,
and not just because he never
says: "You've had one too many"!

He likes to put it this way:
"There's three types of barman,
them that can count and them that can't."


3. The Brand

Growing up was a kitchen clock
ticking *Time For Tennants,*
tea-towels on a washing-line
whistling *Mabel, Black Label,*
milk in a tall glass arguing
*A Guinness Is Good For You,*
sums coming out with pencils stamped
*A Double Diamond Works Wonders,*
a mirror promising *You Can Take*
*A White Horse Anywhere,*
two china dogs beside the fire
answering to *Black & White,*
parents always telling you *Don't*
*Be Vague, Ask For Haig,*
and a hotline to The Pope of Rome:
*Vat 69.*

# The Old Religion

1. Snow Blind

The whole road to Midnight Mass
we pelted each other with the stuff,
two-hand scoops from the tops of cars
kneaded to baseball hardness;
catching breath on narrow boards,
boot toecaps in melted puddles,
pleasure-pain of chilblain knuckles
pressed to chapped lips, whispering:
"Who's the new girl in the white"?
Just a smile would send us flying
through the nave to march hi-ho
along the letters GLORIA IN
EXCELSIS DEO roped above
The Rails in cotton wool.


2.  School Retreat

A three-day furlough from school-work,
mealtime mouthing "milk" and "honey",
and hanging on their polished words,
Redemptorists or Passionists;
which ones had the wooden hearts
(like Elvis) clattering on their chests?
A library of rough-cut texts,
martyrdom and missionary zeal,
Tom Dooley Saving The Free World.
The contents of The Question Box,
like Fatima, at last revealed:

"Father, how far can you go with a girl"?
Half-grateful for the stock reply:
"I once went as far as Cork"!


3. Catechism

I think again to live
ruled by the red and black:
the Six Commandments of The Church,
knowing that Extreme Unction gives
the grace to die right well;
that my son can pick a flower
from the river-bank, close-watched
by a film star Guardian Angel
who will keep him from all harm
and show up in the final frame –
a hasty, stone-built altar,
kindling for the flames,
my God-fearing eyes and that nick-
of-time stay on my arm.


4. The Creator of The Troubles

When full five pounds of meteorite
holed the roof of an RUC Station
and no one claimed responsibility
I saw His hand – not to mention
His manual, King James / Rheims-Douay,
First Lessons in The Dirty War
in versions sized to fit the purse.
(Joshua tumbling neighbours' walls,
the jawbone of an ass that sprayed

the Lounge Bar). Who forced Lucifer
to carry the Big Bang inside
the centre of the Universe
and give the panicked particles
three minutes to get out?

# All My Eye

A sailor entering a foreign church
misheard a supplicant in earnest prayer
to her best friend and comforter-at-hand:
*Ah! mihi, beate Martine* ... (Ah! grant
me, Blessed Martin ...) On making land
in Blighty, he rendered this as *all my eye
and Betty Martin* or, in short, nonsense.

Which would have riled my best-loved maiden aunt:
The Blessed (now Saint) Martin Magazine –
her favourite read – of God's good recompense,
where none who sought would be left in the lurch;
I know they're bound to make a lively pair
in *conversazione* now on high
and Betty Martin nowhere to be seen.

# Around the Village Pump

Long, long ago, a hundred years or more
The House was haunted by something malign;
smashed crockery, a dark stain on the floor,
the dogs upset, a chilling of the spine…
In truth, no governess or parlour maid
would last more than a week beneath that roof;
The minister's best efforts were repaid
in added frenzy. After this reproof
in desperation they approached the priest:
by dint of prayers and Holy Water thrown
he cast 'it' out and all the bother ceased
(it's buried underneath the entrance stone!)
A likely yarn? In grateful recognition
The chapel sits today in prime position.

But whether this is true is hard to say:
A backdoor knock, a voice beyond the light:
"Pack up your family, Andy, don't delay
The Boys intend to 'blow' The Hall tonight
– mind, not a word of this to any others!"
But, here's a thought to keep them occupied:
between them and The Orange Hall live neighbours
and lifelong friends, but from 'the other side'.
So, how does this Greek tragedy unfold?
Someone will surely moot: "We'll say our prayers".
How many times the rosary beads are told
before they sleep still kneeling at their chairs?
The power of prayer, or just a made-up story?
The Hall still stands, in all its made-up glory.

The focus in this last tale is more sharp,
two Christian names give the game away:

the first Paddy, maker of the harp,
the other Samuel, garage-man at play,
his garage walls made of row on row
of old matchboxes; how with 'vroom' and 'beep'
he'd drive his Dinky toy cars in below
Bryant & May, Swan Vesta and Bo Peep.
The harp was made 'inside', in Crumlin Jail,
of hundreds, maybe thousands, of small bits
of used matchsticks sent in to him by mail,
spent hero of the 'fifties bombing blitz:
a careless match, or revenant campaign,
could send the whole place up in smoke again.

# Memoir

From eyebrow to highbrow

From night feed to night club

From baptismal font to Baskerville font

From Biggles to bagels

From hedge school to hedge fund

From First Communion to Credit Union

From Bisto to bistro

From Osmiroid to haemorrhoid

From shamrock to glam rock

From Alice Liddell to Alles Lidl

From James Bond to Prize Bond

From Ringo Starr to Star Bingo

From broad bean to broadband

From royalty cheque to reality check

From scrapbook to scrapheap

# II

'The famous eye will now put on her glasses'
—Elizabeth Bishop

# From The F.X. Buckley Collection

1. *Study of a Woman in Dark Glasses* by George Potter

She could be just the gal next door,
the jolly font of summer lore.
Or maybe those dark glasses hide
the secrets of a battered bride.
In another time and space she stands
upon New Mexico's White Sands
to witness twenty kilotons
shine brighter than a thousand suns.


2. *The Last to Fly* by Graham Knuttel

The tide is out for Mr Punch,
the children all gone home for lunch.
Alone and clearly somewhat vexed
he tries his hand at sending text;
marooned upon this foreign shore
he flags his silent semaphore:
England Expects (so cold, so moody)
That Every Man Will Do His Judy.


3. *Susanna and Elders* by Daniel O'Neill

Thunder and lightning, it's no laugh
when sweet Susanna takes a bath
and just because she won't play ball
these two old Peeping Toms will haul

her up before the local beak
but, Praise Be, Daniel's there to speak
on her behalf, to their discord:
Susanna walks, in the way of The Lord.

# The Boy and the Caravaggio

*i.m. Alex Montwill*


19 Fitzwilliam Place is where
the refugee can earn his keep
by hauling coal up several steep
staircases; and all too aware
of the painting over the mantelpiece
in the doctor's waiting room, he must
be careful not to raise up dust.
O we can guess what this boy sees:
The soldiers! Boyish sense of play,
noting the armour, wants to don
coal-scuttle helmet, poker sword.
But not the boy under the hay
who waits for the soldiers to move on,
his father's whispered "Not a word!"

# The Cross of Cong

*i.m. James MacCullagh 1809 – 1847*

A cross to bear a piece of The True Cross,
oak-cored, embellished with gold filigree;
some craftsman courted eye-strain to emboss
the founding names of Prelate and Ard Rí.

Long centuries of candle-lit procession
have dwindled to a solitary friar,
upon whose death the parish gains possession
and hawks it to the youthful city buyer.

One hundred guineas of his private wealth
establishing a national collection;
a brilliant mind, who suffered much ill health
of that same mind: how deep the disaffection

when he can bear no longer his own cross.
Admire the gift, commemorate the loss.

# To Seamus Heaney in Heaven

When word came I was midway
in a letter to yourself …
"What's he after now?" you ask.
I had begun like Kavanagh's swan,
'head low with many apologies',
like Hamilton writing to Wordsworth:
*Occiditque legendo!*
And keeping to the last
the joke I knew you would enjoy,
the one about the Greek tailor:
Euripides? Eumenides?
But you were already beyant, like Gunnar
sharing poems with The Greats:
Miłosz, Brodsky, Lowell, Hughes, Yeats.

# Air

### 1. Elements

*i.m. John Fitzpatrick*

First earth; The Big Field
in the shadow of the jail
and your eye-hand command
of *sliotar* and *camán*.
Then water; you who never
ran away from anything
planted your oar at Pompey
in the belly of the whale.
And fire; older and wiser
back among the city's
embers of buses and bars,
a phoenix from the ashes
finding air; its buoyancy
tempered by beautiful noise.


### 2. Highwire

This cutting from The Anglo Celt
about a meeting of the Land League –
*So many of Glan's tenant farmers*
*were crowded into the old hayloft*
*that the floor gave way beneath them –*
might raise a smile, the first split
in the movement?
The language is non-committal:
some breakages could equally mean

hay-rakes or brittle bones;
and those who were left hanging
– if not together, then separately? –
the parish stepping out without
a safety net.


3. Gannet

Casing the joint
The Big Top sky
focusing eye
vanishing point

Star circus act
trapeze of air
wing and a prayer
Faustian pact

Spot-lighted sway
music up loud
wave to the crowd
must look away

Icarine fool
gravity's grip
plummeting trip
exploding pool

Kamikaze
moonman return
only concern
next matinee.

# Rathlin Haiku

The ferry *Raasay*:
Walking from Ballycastle
like an Egyptian

~

Manor House parlour:
Baby grand resounding in
a buried horse-head

~

The ruined kelp house
keeps a roof over ghost heads;
old Chemistry set

~

The axe factory:
Stiff foreign competition;
the workforce laid off

~

The disused windmills,
Conn, Fiachra, Aedh O'Lir;
Golgotha of air

~

Waders graze the shore,
advance–retire, dancing to
the beat of the moon

~

The flashing West Light:
Puffins just a memory;
the thirty-nine steps

~

The flashing East Light:
Counting one-two-three-four, go!
Breakout to the pub

~

McCuaig's Bar & Lounge:
A whispering gallery
between these four walls

~

The ferry *Canna:*
Turn whisky into whiskey
For the parting glass

# Radio

1. Marconi on Rathlin Island

He is twenty-four and his first patent
*A wireless system using Hertzian waves*
is barely two years old when Lloyds of London
commissions a radio link across the sound,
their weather eye on transatlantic trade.

He dines with royals while George Kemp along
with Edwin Glanville, Dublin graduate,
and local man John Cecil set up shop
at Ballycastle and Rathlin's East Light.

He makes a four-day visit to the scene
of yet another conquest of the ether,
a triumph turned to dust with Glanville's fall
down some sea cliff to meet an early grave.
They are within a year the same young age.


2. Crystal Set

The single Bakelite headphone
was smuggled into boarding school
in a dayboy's lunchbox;
the red-nosed diode was stretched across
its brass terminals, likewise two curls
of electrical flex.
If you crouched down in the dormitory
for the radiator's pipework 'earth'
while your own body's saline aerial

completed the simple circuit,
you could catch the plummy voice:
*This is the BBC Home Service...*
Lone yachtsman tethered to the mast,
buoyed up by the Shipping Forecast.


3. The Mystery Sound

No, it's not the start-up tone
of a mobile phone,
nor chalk being scored
across a school blackboard,
nor the scrape of a half-door
on a cottage flagstone floor,
nor the high-speed drilling
of a dental filling,
nor the mating-call
of the (never heard of it!) quetzal,
nor (though it's close) the opening note
of Joseph and the Amazing Technicolour Dreamcoat.
No, none of you got this one
but isn't that all part of the fun?
The answer was ... a human scream
– one of mine, it would seem:
Call us if you find that sordid;
this programme was pre-recorded.

# No Second Glance

My fiftieth birthday
finds me living in a college
among young undergraduates
'bright of eye, bushy of tail'
to whom without a shadowed doubt
I am invisible:
I've dusted off my father's coat
his woollen gloves, his old trilby
and raided Matron's cabinet
for extra-length white winding bandage
to cover me from Adam's apple
to thinning crown, shades on peepholes;
at the first inquisitive looks
I'll slip into some telephone box.

# Love

1. The Request

Write me a real love poem, she said,
not one of your trademark ironies;
from the heart this time, not the head.

The thirty-plus years we've been wed
weigh in with this request to, please,
write me a real love poem; she said,

no talk of paths we've yet to tread,
no hint of shared eternities;
from the heart this time, not the head.

No squint-eyed Cupid's arrow sped,
no corny jokes, no schmalz, no cheese;
write me a real love poem, she said,

no murmurings of 'how love fled …'
no airy-fairy sophistries;
from the heart this time, not the head.

The Olivetti on the bed,
the warm caress of well-worn keys;
write me a real love poem, she said,
from the heart this time, not the head.

## 2. Parodies Lost

*i.m. Dennis O'Driscoll*

Love set you going like a fat gold watch
Checked by the referee, to start the match

How do I love thee? Let me count the ways
There's hugging, kissing, biting and swapping jerseys

Yes, injured Woman! Rise, assert thy right
Or did you take a dive, when out of sight?

Because I could not stop for Death
I was substituted, out of breath

Oh where are you going with your love-locks flowing
The offside flag is up, the whistle blowing

I, being born a woman and distressed
I lost the chance to score when dispossessed

I was much further out than you thought
And not saving your backheader, as I ought

The art of losing isn't hard to master
It's easy when the other team is faster

The mind is an enchanting thing
That's why supporters always sing

To sing of wars, of captains and of kings
And, most of all, the season's new signings

I think very well of Susan but I do not know her name
Soccer is a bit like Poetry, it's a funny old game

## 3. Leaving the Golden Hind

Wrapped in our families' affairs
like Drake's men, afraid
to wash away all the good luck
of carnations and new hats.

Our threats and taunts are cannon-shot
through the rigging of the fitted kitchen,
red quarry tiles masking the drip
from a thousand tiny cuts.

Before they toss us overboard,
bundled up in our high tog duvet,
somebody should think about
jumping ship.

# III

'Les yeux sont le miroir de l'âme'
—French proverb

# Pupil

I know the pupil of the eye dilates
according to the loss of ambient glow;
the pupil, properly an empty space,
a framing of the window of the soul,
may also register astonishment;
as my own must have done, I realize,
reading on Wikipedia (to my shame)
something new that Every Boy Should Know
concerning the humanity of eyes:
that sexual arousal does the same.
But waking in the night and face to face
stare right into the maw of twin Black Holes
is tantamount to angering The Fates,
to risk collapse of this dark firmament.

# Second Chance

Keep an eye for my Box Number
in the latest Personal Columns
of The Dunsinane Telegraph:
'Twiddling pricked thumbs?
Well-read, good sense of humour,
Mac seeks a better half'.
Someone who will understand
the kind of man I might have been
before it all got out of hand,
the hurly-burly madcap waltz,
losing the trick of how to win
while never, ever playing false:
'Likes to take long walks across the heather,
wittering on about the bloody weather'.

# Nightmare in The Women's Hall of Residence

Always to observe this ritual:
First, appraise the contents of the room,
the narrow bed, the shape familiar,
the grubby poster-board, pockmarked with pins.
Second, take a purifying shower
and towel-dry with care the sacred parts,
(the omphalos and under the foreskin).
Third, cross-legged on the carpet, trim
the toenails, saving each small crescent moon
to make a life-preserving pentacle:
Do this or else that coven of old crones
(your student loves) will summon their Black Arts
to pluck your eyes out, tear you limb from limb
and suck the marrow from your Freshman bones.

# Time

## 1. They Also Serve

The tuatara lodged in Invercargill,
their stock as old as some proverbial hill,
will also boast a socket in the skull

in which to host a pineal third eye
with lens and retina, which may be why
the über-centenarian male that they

have christened Henry (after Henry Jones?)
has sensed a gleam between the parietal bones
of Mildred, eighty-odd – erogenous zones

are only half the battle for a mate,
time matters too; for you who stand and wait
it's never, as the old song goes, too late.


## 2. On The DART

It's never the night-mail crossing the border
bringing the cheque... nor the nasal wheel whine
of wee Lonnie Donegan's Rock Island Line;
nor does it ever play host to a murder,

ze leetle grey cells on The Orient-Express
or two complete strangers hatching a plot;
nor a session with Sugar in Some Like It Hot,
hiding the bourbon flask under her dress.

It's very unlikely that someone will call
"Are ye right there, Michael?" or that you might
have your own Brief Encounter on some lonely night.
It is none of these things, but it could be them all

as you give yourself up at the end of the day
to the 3.10 to Yuma, the 6.12 to Bray.


3. A Dangling Conversation

All he remembers of War & Peace
is the princess with the downy lip...
though thankfully not a harelip!
Yet, wasn't there a famous Herr Lip,
the maker of the best French watch
till competition shut the plant
and the operation was wound up,
leaving the workers quite ticked off
and looking for the big handout,
being strapped for cash, especially
the one with a second loan on the house
wondering how he'd tell the wife:
"O Princess, have you got a minute...?"
and planning to while away the hours
re-reading War & Peace.

# Colour

### 1. Protanopia

With 'red' cones missing in your spectral sight
there's no discriminating blue from purple.
More worrying, that tricky traffic light
might leave you with a lifelong need to hirple.

### 2. Deuteranopia

The chemist Dalton first logged this defect,
himself afflicted by poor 'green' supply:
A century and a half proved him correct
through DNA from his preserved left eye.

### 3. Tritanopia

Here yellow's indistinguishable from pink
with indigo and blue in paucity:
Because there is no chromosomal link
this is a case of sex equality.

### 4. Achromatopsia

Meanwhile upon the isle of Pingelap,
thanks to the 1780 storm, they say,
the odds are greatly shortened that a chap
might see the world in fifty shades of grey.

# At The Garden Pier, Atlantic City

*i.m. Rick Heiden*

*When Irish Eyes … Oft in the Stilly Night …*
McCormack's tenor soared above the swell
to carry like a child's newspaper kite
as far as The Imperial Hotel.
But concerts and sandcastles dwindle down
and there's a different kind of carnival
as punters and high rollers hit the town
in Caesar's, Showboat and Trump Taj Mahal.
When, counter-culture in their midst, the pier's
the venue for some poetry, I caught
your pure-delighting stage-whisper of *Geez!*
at mention of my son's girlfriends & beers:
I marked the moment but how little thought
it bounden to the cruel ocean breeze.

# Music

1. Two Choirs

May morn on Magdalen Tower roof
and more, this glorious 'wall of sound'
barricading St John's Quad,
mortarboards floating past the lodge.
I would have them chant a dirge
for Miss Gunne, cruelly marooned
in our church choirloft, the joys
of twenty-odd pitch-challenged 'crows'
belting out the *Tantum Ergo:*
every Christmas our reward –
wee paper-pokes of *Danny Boys*
(the end of more than one eye tooth).
The 'Derry Air then let them sing:
The organ pipes are caw-aw-ling!

## 2. Hammer Horror

When I read of the uilleann pipes
the professor willed to be interred
in his own grave, "Well," I averred,
"It takes all types …"

But then a rival prof took heart
and had the ancient pipes exhumed
in order, it must be assumed,
to save a dying art.

Late last night I followed my nose
until I discovered the basement bed
of the grisly, triple-horned undead
and as the moon rose

(and purely for music's sake)
I hammered home the stake.

# Horse

### 1. Evolution

The nictitans, or third eyelid, perforce
a T-shaped piece of hyaline cartilage,
has been the windscreen wiper to the horse
since many moons before the horseless carriage.

### 2. Predestination

The golden horseshoe graven
On a tombstone in Clonmel:
The stable door of Heaven?
The smithy fire of Hell?

### 3. The Poet Loses His Shirt on Yeats
*(Melbourne Cup 2006)*

That is no country for old nags,
no Gucci shoes and Prada bags
nor public men, nor cheering crowds
could save my horse from eating clouds
of others' dust in his defeat,
as he treads softly with clay feet.
Why should I blame him that he filled
my heart with sorrow, while others thrilled?
Though I am old with wandering
I'll face the future pondering
he might have won fame in the end

had he but taken that first bend ...
Salt was the tear in this cold eye
as he let each horseman pass by!

# Yeats Country

*for Sheila O'Hagan*

### 1. The Tower

I, the poet Iggy Mac,
made pilgrimage to view this stack
of sticks & stones & iron but,
it being Autumn, all was shut;
new phone books clogged the door; the age is
writ in dog-eared Yellow Pages.

### 2. The Lake

The wild swans at Coole
are calm as a rule,
patrolling the shore
like any Booth-Gore;
they float side by side
like any Lees-Hyde;
no wave-like dispersion
disturbs their inversion.

### 3. The Autograph Tree

I think that I will never see
my own initials on *that* tree!

# Ulymericks

Buck Mulligan, plump and statelee,
rags Stephen whose Mum's RIP;
the tower's a kip
Buck goes for a dip
in the scrotumtightening sea.

~

'Sir' Stephen shows weary regard
for someone who finds sums too hard;
his foot in his mouth
old Deasy's uncouth
to our bullockbefriending bard.

~

Ineluctable modality
plus a shaggy dog fatality;
a bilingual rant
la Plume de ma Tante?
a nose-picking finality.

~

Inner organs of beasts and fowls,
a letter from Blazes, Bloom scowls;
its import denied,
a kidney is fried;
an effortless movement of bowels.

~

A letter from Martha, Bloom's joy
is tempered by meeting McCoy;
no rent for the Pope,
buy lotion and soap,
a flower for one naughty boy

~

A road-race to quicken the dead
and put Paddy Dignam to bed;
Parnell, the old fox,
is not in his box;
he died of a Tuesday, 'tis said

~

Fresh from omnium gatherums
of Nelson's and Freeman's columns,
our Stephen is led
to the boosing shed
by the Parable of the Plums.

~

While gastronome Leopold spurns
The Burton for chic Davy Byrne's
gorgonzola and red
wine gone to the head,
to the Library by about-turns.

~

Where Stephen has taken the floor
to lecture on cold Elsinore;
the last Will is read
on second-best bed
then *Exeunt All* out the door.

~

Father Conmee, the Dignam boy
and the (doublin') hoi polloi
criss-cross in the street,
some Dedali meet;
all strain to salute The Viceroy.

~

Two barmaids discuss cons and pros
of marriage to 'the greasy nose';
by cider and Powers
there's more talk of flowers
and somebody sings *The Last Rose*.

~

The Heroes of Ireland crowd in
the court of RM Citizen;
maligned as a cheat
Bloom's forced to retreat,
pursued by a dog-biscuit-tin.

~

While Gerty conceives of astriction,
the strains of Retreat Benediction
cross Sandymount Strand;
self taken in hand
limply Bloom will mark her affliction.

~

A visit to Mrs Purefoy;
Some medics press Bloom to enjoy
full many a glass
of Number One Bass;
to Burke's, at the news of a boy.

~

Nightsdream about women and wine
enlivened by costume design;
the leg of a duck
earns Stephen a puck:
The Horse has the neigh-saying line.

~

A refuge from Cissies and malt,
The Cabman's night shelter their halt;
S.D. will have none
of coffee and bun
nor Bloom the tall tales of a salt.

~

Bloom, keyless, climbs over the gate,
relief as they co-urinate;
tell-tale potted meat
on fresh linen sheet
where Blazes has shifted his weight.

~

Now Molly's awake in the bed
with lots of bad thoughts in her head;
to finish she'll say
sure, fine, right, okay,
henceforth, you can take that as read!

# IV

'I tooke a bodkine & put it betwixt my eye & [the] bone'
—Isaac Newton

# The Eyes of Isaac Newton

Let us salute the oddest of them all,
who used a bodkin to investigate
how pressure might affect his own eyeball
yet came down on the right of the debate
that sight is 'intromittist' – light received
and not that light from their captains' piercing eyes
caused soldiers to shield theirs, as was believed
by the ancient Greeks who would philosophize
upon the origins of that salute –
and that this light was made up of corpuscles
(a flyball that Einstein would one day catch),
then played the private eye in hot pursuit
of Chaloner; their last of many tussles
would see the coiner's bulging-eyed dispatch.

# Crossing The Uncanny Valley

When word spread throughout our northern town
that the mannequins in the Church Street draper's window
left nothing to the imagination, down
to the smallest anatomical detail,
we let our eyes long linger in a slow
descent from perfect snowy peaks of breast
or rise up leggy heights we'd yet to scale …
then coming to a disconcerting rest

at another window, in a southern city,
on Patrick Street where once seafaring Russians
left high and dry on "No Drink!" Christmas Day
had posed for photos with the almost human;
the firm embrace of cold prosthetic clay,
the smiling warmth of their enduring pity.

# Motoring

## 1. At The National Car Test Centre

Free of gender, race or creed,
shorn of your hubcaps' proud dressage,
you humbly surrender book and key
then pace the forecourt, praying for
– no tell-tale rattle of the shocks
no whiff of duff katalysator –
just the grateful Yea.

So shall it be on The Last Day,
when horns will summon up the dead,
sheep or goat in separate flocks
as His eye scans your Judgement Page,
yet buoyed-up by the quickfire rumour
that, this time round, adultery
don't matter.

## 2. Oisin

My favourite cousin Pat
drags his bad knee over the gears
of an ancient tractor:

The instant that his boot
touches the gravel we'll subtract "Oh,
nigh on three-score years".

## 3. Deceleration

In Ledbury churchyard
lies someone
named Sixty, gone
to his reward
– so far, and yet so near –
in his fifty-ninth year!
O Lord, forgive the gall
of this two-bit cheap shot:
Sixty to nought
in no time at all.

# Science

1. Twins

They were something
out of the ordinary;
two peas in a pod,
eye-dent-eye-cal.

Whose idea
to separate them
and strike one
to watch both cry?

That was the year
I mastered fractions:
numerator,
denominator

and I finally pierced the pother,
distinguishing one from the other.


2. The Lesson

*after Miroslav Holub*

The students ask:
What is the colour of the neutrino?
The teacher smiles:
This question has no answer.
The students protest:
If the question can be asked

there must be an answer, even one
that teacher doesn't know!
When the school-bell rings for lunch
lock it away with all the others:
What is the lifetime of an idea?
What is the electron spin of love?
What is the wavelength of the soul?
What the rest mass of death?

3. Lab Notes

The burner that still bears his name
belies a price too high:
The journey on the road to fame
cost Bunsen his right eye.

When Roentgen took the first X-ray
of his dear wife's left hand,
he noted, much to his dismay,
how loose was her gold band.

The fly in the cathedral flew
crisscross that mighty room.
Then settled on an empty pew
and softly whispered "Boom!"

# Quantum Clerihew

Max Planck
is the man to thank
for the mysterious phantom
that is the quantum.

~

Louis de Broglie
had the unholy
idea that a moving particle
was not a definite article.

~

Werner Heisenberg
would not waste an erg
on those who were not convincible
about his uncertainty principle.

~

Albert Einstein
liked to opine:
"It's not very nice
Of God to play dice!"

~

Erwin Schrödinger
Had the eye of a swinger.
His eponymous wave equation, it's said
was conceived in a mystery woman's bed.

~

Paul Dirac
took a different tack.
People thought he was mad as a hatter
with his prediction of antimatter.

~

Neils Bohr
might feel sore
if he heard my brother's perceptive remark:
Something rotten in the state of the theory of Denmark.

# His Cat

A place, you could say, where a thought might grow
*Gedankenexperiment*, this stout sealed box
admits no view and yet the world would know
its drama well before they spring the locks.

More famous even than Unsinkable Sam,
Black Beauty, Lassie, Skippy, Mickey Mouse
or Laika The Astrodog or Shrek The Ram,
I am your guide around this haunted house:

Here is the Geiger tube that will contain
a radioactive source so low in power
one atom can decay or yet refrain
with *equal* chance within a chosen hour.

The rest is easy, should there be decay
some circuitry will trigger the response
of this old-fashioned solenoid relay
to set that hammer falling and at once

smash this small phial of a deadly gas.
Until your look-see moment will arrive
things must remain at this surreal impasse:
I am absurdly both dead and alive!

But four score years have tempered my unease
With cartoons drawn on T-shirts by the dozen
And jokes galore, of which the best of these:
Schrödinger's cat walks into a bar – and doesn't.

# Walking the Dog

Too many hours together
nosing out of the undergrowth
more than our share of abandoned babies,
our quota of hooded reprisals,
our ration of underwear.

At the scrape of a kitchen chair
or the tell-tale clink of the leash
where once was a whirlwind of delight
he shrinks into the shadows,
avoiding my eye.

p. 11: Hypermetropia is a condition of the eye that causes close objects to appear blurred, while far objects may appear normal; it is commonly referred to as long-sightedness or far-sightedness.

p. 27: Three of the paintings from the F.X. Buckley Collection of modern art, which may be viewed in The Irish Writers Centre at No. 19 Parnell Square, Dublin.

p. 29: The painting *The Taking of Christ* by Michelangelo Caravaggio was at one stage in the ownership of Irish paediatrician, Marie Lea-Wilson; the physicist Alex Montwill came to Ireland as a child refugee and was sponsored by Dr Lea-Wilson. The painting is now in The National Gallery in Dublin.

p. 30: The Cross of Cong was for many centuries in the care of the Augustinian Abbey in Cong, Co. Galway. It was purchased by Professor MacCullagh of Trinity College in the 1830s; the gifted mathematician took his own life in 1847. The Cross of Cong is now in the National Museum of Ireland in Dublin.

p. 31: The mathematician William Rowan Hamilton employed the Latin phrase *Occiditque legendo* in a letter to William Wordsworth in connection with the many poems he was enclosing; if the origin of the phrase is Horace, his likely meaning is that the recipient will be exhausted by reading same.

p. 40: The couplets in 'Parodies Lost' borrow from the works of eleven women poets: readers who wish to test their knowledge of these might (in TV football parlance) "look away now". The poets are listed at the end of these notes*.

p. 48: The tuatara is a reptile that comes from the dinosaur era, and is only found in the wild on some protected offshore islands of New Zealand; in 2009 a tuatara couple bred in captivity (and in longevity!) at the Southland Museum in the South Island town of Invercargill.

p. 48: DART is the acronym for Dublin Area Rapid Transit.

p. 50: The three main forms of colour-deficiency are protanopia, deuteranopia and tritanopia, corresponding to deficiency of 'red', 'green' and 'blue', respectively. Achromatopsia is total colour-blindness; like protanopia and deuteranopia, it is a male chromosomal defect and its preponderance in Pingelap is attributed to the survival of one dominant male with that condition.

p. 55: Yeats is an Irish thoroughbred racehorse, the only horse to win the Ascot Gold Cup four times in succession. He is named after the poet's brother, the painter Jack B. Yeats.

p. 57: 'Ulymericks' reflects a hurried first reading of Joyce's masterpiece.

p. 66: 'The uncanny valley' is a hypothesis in the field of aesthetics, which holds that when features look and move almost, but not exactly, like natural beings, it causes a response of revulsion among some observers. The "valley" refers to the dip in a graph of comfort versus similarity.

p. 70: The fly in question is the atomic nucleus, which was, in the early days of its discovery, compared in size with the whole atom as a fly compares to a cathedral.

*Sylvia Plath, Elizabeth Barrett Browning, Anna Laetitia
Barbauld, Emily Dickinson, Christina Rossetti, Edna St
Vincent Millay, Stevie Smith, Elizabeth Bishop, Marianne
Moore, Anne Bradstreet, and Gertrude Stein.

Lightning Source UK Ltd.
Milton Keynes UK
UKHW01f1656070518
322235UK00001B/263/P